How To Buy A Small Business And Let The Government Finance It

Robert E. Seng

authorHOUSE®

AuthorHouse™
1663 Liberty Drive
Bloomington, IN 47403
www.authorhouse.com
Phone: 1-800-839-8640

First published by AuthorHouse   1/23/2010

ISBN: 978-1-4490-4862-4 (hc)
ISBN: 978-1-4490-4861-7 (sc)
ISBN: 978-1-4490-4860-0 (e)

Printed in the United States of America
Bloomington, Indiana

This book is printed on acid-free paper.

How to Buy a Small Business
(And Let the Government Help Finance It)

Acknowledgements

My years have taught me that very seldom do you accomplish difficult things entirely alone. You receive inspiration and, education from some, and actual physical assistance from yet another group. It is with this thought in mind that I acknowledge my debt to the following: Emmy Seng for her constant inspiration and love, my daughters Lizabeth Drinkwine and Laurie Rainey, who always loved me and thought I was bigger than life and nicknamed me "The Giant", E. S. "Ned" Dewey who taught me a great deal of what I know about Small Business, Jim Callahan who believed in me and always remained my friend, my wife Becky Seng who constantly urged me to complete this book and gave me the love to accomplish it and Patti Space for her assistance in editing, and to the hundreds of others who contributed to my experience and knowledge.

How to Buy a Small Business
(And Let the Government Help Finance It)

How to Buy a Small Business
(And Let the Government Help Finance It)

How to Buy a Small Business
(And Let the Government Help Finance It)

Introduction

So you want to buy a small business? You've decided, though, that you don't want to follow the same path as most people. You've analyzed the situation and decided that working for others is not the best way to financial security, and that you don't want to always work for others. Instead, you would like to be in charge of your own destiny.

When you were growing up, you were told that the way to develop your future was to get an education, a job with a good company, work all your life, and save a little money. Finally, you retire and plan to live out your life in comfort, the "American dream." It used to work that way for some but not anymore. The truth is out for those who see the real situation. Our fathers worked for companies that kept them working all their life and retired them when they got old. Today's companies don't have that same kind of loyalty, and the marketplace will no longer allow them to keep employees who don't produce at the maximum.

Only about five percent of retirees can maintain the same standard of living they have before retirement. The other ninety-five percent who dream of a "carefree" retirement are now surprised to learn that over the years inflation has reduced their spendable income. The pension they now have for their lifetime of work is too small, and even coupled with Social Security and savings, the nest egg can't keep pace with rising prices for food, clothing, gasoline, automobiles, and housing

"Carefree retirement" is now anything but carefree. Many who are forced to retire suddenly have seen their lifestyle deteriorate into struggle and despair—a rather inglorious end to a distinguished working career.

How to Buy a Small Business
(And Let the Government Help Finance It)

This common story demonstrates that for most of us you can't rely on your employer, the government, or anyone else to take care of you when you retire; you have to take care of yourself.

If you consider people who are truly able to enjoy their retirement in relative financial security, you would probably learn that most of them worked for themselves. They did it on their own. Be it just good fortune or a keen eye for reality, these folks knew that they had to take care of themselves, and that there was no such thing as a "free lunch."

Another problem with working for someone else is you either become too old to perform to your employer's satisfaction or there is a mandatory retirement age, where you might not have achieved the financial security you need for retirement. What if you want to keep working? You are probably going to have to start all over, working for a new company, and learning a new system, if you're lucky.

When you own your own business, you never have to retire; you can own the business until you die. If later in life you can't work full-time, you can hire someone to replace you and continue to own the business and derive an income from it. There are many possible scenarios, but they can all lead to having an income from the business for as long as you live.

Longevity has improved. Years ago, by the time someone retired, it was almost time to die. In the 1950s, the average life span was 67 years for males, and if you retired at 65 you only lived two years after retirement. Back then, things were different. You didn't need vast sums of money for all the wonderful retirement activities we have today. Life was simple and costs were low. Today, people live twenty to thirty years after retirement, and that requires not only a pension and Social Security but also, in many cases, a substantial amount of cash. But what about before retirement?

How to Buy a Small Business
(And Let the Government Help Finance It)

What about the years when you buy a house and furnish it, buy a car or two for the family, send your children to college, and take vacations? This takes a lot of money. Will your boss give it to you? You know the answer.

About 95 percent of people who work hard for someone else for thirty or forty years will rely on inadequate pensions and Social Security for retirement. Most of us know that, but few do something about it. It's human nature to not want to leave the comfort zone.

There comes a time in life when you should consider becoming the "boss," doing what you want, doing what you enjoy. If you should fail, you can always go back to working for someone else, but at least you would know you tried. "It's better to have tried and failed than never to have tried at all."

But since you are reading this little book, I know I'm "preaching to the choir." You know all these things, and now you want some control in your life and be directly responsible for what happens to you and your family. Bravo!

This book is about and for those individuals who have decided to **buy** their own business, but it can also be used by anyone who wants to start a business. Most of the process that you follow to buy a business is also applicable to starting a business. It is not an attempt to be a literary success. Rather, it is intended to be easily read and understood and serve as a guide you can follow when buying a business—if you want to be successful through your own efforts, earn a substantial living, acquire equity, and create something of value for you and your family.

People who are successful in their own business usually want more in life and will persevere regardless of the obstacles. They don't accept the word "failure," or at least it doesn't scare them.

How to Buy a Small Business
(And Let the Government Help Finance It)

Most successful small-business owners recognize the need for detail and organization. They constantly search for ways to improve their business, to offer new products, make the current product better, and pay particular attention to the quality of their service and product.

Successful business owners usually know their sales, expenses, cost of product, salaries, and inventories, and have a schedule for evaluating each item. Many didn't have all this knowledge when they started in business, but they learned quickly. This same attention to detail and proactive thinking is really needed before buying a business.

Buying a business may be one of the most important decisions you make in your life; it is certainly one of the most costly. This book will outline many of the steps you need to take before and after you buy a small business. I will discuss most of the "due diligence" you should take before making an offer on a business. None of this is difficult to understand, but if it's new for you, don't be discouraged. Part of being a business owner is learning how to learn "on the fly."

Some Important Considerations

It's very important when buying a small business that you buy one in which you have some knowledge or experience. If you have worked in a restaurant for ten years and you buy a hair salon, you face a tremendous learning curve to overcome. Not only do you have to learn the business but you also have to learn how to negotiate with suppliers, how to "speak" the language of a new industry. Learn the "tricks" of the trade and become familiar with how to obtain new customers. It is also important when buying a business to actually like the business.

How to Buy a Small Business
(And Let the Government Help Finance It)

If you insist on buying a business you know nothing about, you should work in that industry until you learn and can find out if you really like the business. If you don't want to spend the time learning a new business, then try to get the current owner to stay and work for you until you do learn.

Owning a business is not the answer to everyone's prayers. Some individuals are not self-motivated, and they don't have a "passion" for the business they are thinking about acquiring. They aren't flexible enough to handle the multiple duties they must perform; they have a problem managing, hiring, teaching, buying, accounting, and taking on other responsibilities of ownership. They don't understand that winners "make it happen."

Successful owners are constantly learning and improving their operation and in most cases are either good at managing employees or learn how to do so.

My first job was working in a service station. When I first started, my "boss" could not supervise employees very well, so he took a course in employee management.

About a year later, he had occasion to reprimand me for my handling of a customer. He told me, "I think the way you talked to that customer and the service you gave was horrible, and I never want to see or hear you speak to a customer like that again … and what particularly upset me is you're so good at everything else you do."

How could I be mad at him, when he tells me that I'm good at everything I do? I had to believe the criticism was justified if I believed his remarks about my general demeanor. He had successfully learned how to positively "criticize performance" and get the employee to accept the criticism.

Where he had once been poor in managing personnel, through additional education he had become excellent.

Ongoing self-training is essential to being a successful business owner.

Many of the talents you need to be successful in a small business can be learned "on the job"; however, when you start, you need confidence, perseverance, optimism, enthusiasm, and a totally positive vision of being successful. You must not accept the word "failure."

How to Buy a Small Business
(And Let the Government Help Finance It)

<u>Chapter 1: Let's Talk</u>

This book may save you thousands of dollars and many headaches if you decide to buy a small business. Buying a business is a big step, so be sure to prepare yourself before realizing the "dream"; otherwise, it could turn into a nightmare.

Since you were a youngster, you have heard the expressions about freedom: "be your own boss" or "be independent, own your own business." After working for someone else, most of us can identify with these statements. We would love not having to work for anyone else, report to anyone else, work under what we would consider adverse conditions, or be laid off or fired. If you work for yourself, no one will change your hours, no one will supervise your work or tell you how to do it, and no one will be around to ruin your day when they are in a bad mood. What a wonderful world! You are totally independent.

All these statements can be true, provided you take certain steps when buying your business to ensure that you are getting everything you are paying for and not being mislead or deceived by an unscrupulous seller.

<u>An Owner Wears Many Hats</u>

It's important that you consider the tremendous amount of work and time that you must devote to operate and grow your business. In a small business, you're sometimes the President, Sales Manager, Human Resources Manager, Financial Manager, Operations Manager, Computer Expert, Buyer, Customer Service Manager, as well as the Cashier and Janitor. It's a big job with many responsibilities and, in addition, you must be motivated and be a motivator. You should also be able to recruit, train, and motivate new employees. Owning your own business can be a big job, but there are great rewards if you are successful.

How to Buy a Small Business
(And Let the Government Help Finance It)

Know Something About the Business

When buying a small retail business, it's a good idea to know something about the business and to know a lot about yourself. You should buy a business that you have working experience with or one you know very well.

Know Something About Yourself

Also, you need to understand if you are right for the business. In other words, don't buy a business that requires a lot of customer contact if you don't particularly like people. Instead, buy one where you have little or no contact with the public. Some businesses will have both contact and no-contact positions. For example, in the restaurant business, if you enjoy working with people, you can be at the door greeting them, handling service, and satisfying customers. Or, if you prefer, you could be in the kitchen preparing food and have someone else be the greeter.

I know a man who is one of the best jewelry repairmen in the city, but he has absolutely no personality and doesn't like to deal with people. His shop also sells jewelry, so he employs a very talented lady to do the selling, and he confines his duties to inspecting items to be repaired, quoting prices, and repairing the jewelry. He is very successful and has been in business for over fifteen years.

If you don't know anything about the business—get experience before you make a final decision.

As stated previously, one of the easiest ways to fail in a small retail business is to buy one you know nothing about. If you consider such a business, then get a job in that field working for someone else until you have a good "feel" for the business, understand its pluses and minuses, and feel comfortable working in such an environment.

A common way to solve this problem is to make the sale contingent upon the seller staying on long enough to train the new owner. *You, the buyer, retain the right to cancel the sale if you don't fit in or if the business is not what it appeared to be.*

Anecdote #1

In my career of buying and selling businesses, I have seen successes and failures, some of them from inexperience, some from stupidity, and some from lack of good judgment.

In Florida, a man and his wife operated a successful restaurant for over fifteen years, selling salads, soup, and sandwiches. They made fresh chicken, tuna, shrimp, and potato salad every morning.

They arrived at the restaurant at 6 a.m. and started preparing the fresh salads for the lunch and dinner trade. Since they were already at the restaurant preparing menu items for the day, they developed a small breakfast business that was very profitable. Their salads were served with a stick of delicious French bread, which was baked a little at a time to keep it fresh. The soups were a premium canned soup to which they added additional ingredients to make them thicker and tastier.

Their business was very successful for over fifteen years, but when the wife became ill and could no longer work, they decided to sell. The business was purchased by a woman, who had been traveling for a clothing firm. Her son, who had worked in construction, was going to help her.

After about a month in the business, the woman decided that instead of coming in so early in the morning to prepare the salads, they would prepare them the night before and keep them in the refrigerator.

How to Buy a Small Business
(And Let the Government Help Finance It)

Since they now opened later in the morning, the breakfast business disappeared. The salads, having been in the refrigerator all night, did not appear fresh, and each salad took on some of the flavors of the other salads. As business slowed due to the poor quality of the food, the woman and her son decided to cut costs and bought a cheaper French bread that was much inferior to the previous bread. As a result of these changes, the business declined and eventually the woman had to sell it for inventory and lost $100,000.

The lesson here is "If it's not broke, don't fix it." If they had just continued the successful operation they purchased, they would probably still be in business today.

Anecdote # 2

Tony is an excellent chef. His food is delicious, and his presentation is beautiful. When he prepares a meal, it looks so good you can hardly wait to eat it; it is marvelous.

Tony opened a restaurant, and people flocked to it. As time passed, however, his business slowly declined. He couldn't understand why everyone wouldn't come to eat his delicious food. Finally, Tony, with some advice from a consultant, surveyed some of his former clients.

To his surprise, the common answer was "we loved your food, but the service was so poor, we were frustrated by the time we were served." Tony was a talented chef, but he wasn't very good at recruitment, hiring, and training.

He solved his problem by hiring a very talented woman who had a great ability to recruit and motivate employees, and she did a magnificent job of improving service.

When you own a business, you must wear many hats as mentioned earlier. Having a good product is not enough. Successful business owners have to be involved in every facet of their business.

Anecdote # 3

A man once purchased a business in a shopping mall. Only fat-free hot dogs, French fries, and drinks were sold. He had one cook, who didn't need much experience to cook hot dogs and French fries, and one server, who put the food on a plate and gave it to the customer. The owner sat on a stool at the cash register and collected the money.

The business was eventually sold, and the new owner didn't change a thing. For over seven years now, the new owner has had a very successful business and income.

If you buy a successful business, it is usually financially beneficial to not make any substantial changes until you thoroughly understand the business and your customers.

Chapter 2: Know What You're Paying For

Small businesses are sold in various ways, including the following:

1. Listings by owners in newspapers or other media
2. Through friends and associates
3. Contact with a licensed business broker

Using a Business Broker

It is sometimes suggested that one of the best and safest ways to purchase a small business is by having a business broker help negotiate the sale. They are licensed by the state and have to be honest in their dealings or they can lose their license. Generally, they secure a great deal of information from the seller, which saves you time, and they can usually answer many of your questions about the business before you ever have to meet the seller.

Many brokers already have important information about sales, gross profit, expenses, occupancy costs, and terms, as well as financial statements or pro forma statements, and, in some cases, brokers have the actual income tax returns from the business for the last several years. All of this information may not be totally accurate, but at least it is something to verify and gives you a place to start.

It's always best to be armed with the facts before talking to the owner for the first time, and using a business broker is a good way to gather the necessary information before-hand. Many people will tell you that going to a business broker will cost additional money; however, the commission is paid by the seller, and your broker should ensure that the eventual sales price represents a fair market price for the business.

When you have all the information you need before meeting with the seller, it makes you a more "qualified buyer" and prepares you to ask more intelligent questions. First impressions are usually lasting, and you should make it a point to be prepared and proactive in your business dealings.

Many people who buy a small business and particularly if it is their first business tend to be so enthusiastic that they fail to adequately protect themselves. A broker can help reduce the emotion and help guide you through the many "due diligence" steps that must be followed.

While it is true that most small businesses can provide an excellent income, benefits and security, there is never a guarantee. If not handled correctly from the start, most businesses can also produce anxiety, frustration, and heartache. Using a business broker can help avoid making mistakes in this critical and expensive decision.

The Burden Is On The Buyer

The burden is always on the buyer to examine a business thoroughly and satisfy themselves that they are getting what they are paying for. It is the responsibility of the buyer to substantiate the sales, expenses, and income associated with the business, as well as many other items that will be identified in future chapters.

Although many sellers are honest, the best policy is always to assume nothing and adhere to the old axiom "buyer beware."

The following chapters will give you a blueprint to follow in buying your small retail business. Follow them and you can be assured that you will be well prepared for what you are about to buy.

Chapter 3: Basic Financial Statements

If done properly, financial statements are like a laboratory analysis for doctors in making a diagnosis of what is really happening beneath the surface.

The financial "numbers" can indicate how solvent (Balance Sheet) and how profitable (Operating Statement) a company is. These two financial statements, along with a Cash Flow Statement, are the three reports you, your broker, and your accountant must see before considering the purchase of a business.

If a company doesn't have at least a balance sheet and an operating statement, you should be very skeptical and make this information a contingency in any potential purchase.

The Balance Sheet

A balance sheet represents a company's financial position for *one day* during its fiscal year—for example, the last day of its accounting period, which can differ from the more familiar calendar year. Companies typically select an ending period that corresponds to a time when their business activities have reached the lowest point in their annual cycle, which is referred to as their natural business year.

How the Balance Sheet Works

The balance sheet is divided into two parts that, based on the following equation, must equal (or balance out) each other. The main formula behind balance sheets is as follows:

$$\text{Assets} = \text{Liabilities} + \text{Shareholders' Equity}$$

This means that assets, or the means used to operate the company, are balanced by a company's financial obligations, along with the equity investment brought into the company and any retained earnings.

Assets are what a company uses to operate its business, while its liabilities and equity are two sources that support these assets. Owners' equity, also referred to as shareholders' equity in a publicly traded company, is the amount of money initially invested in the company plus any retained earnings, and it represents a source of funding for the company.

It is important to note that a balance sheet is a snapshot of the company's *financial position at a single point in time.*

Types of Assets

Current Assets

Current assets have a life span of one year or less, meaning they can be easily converted into cash. Asset classes are cash and cash equivalents, accounts receivable, and inventory. Cash, the most fundamental of current assets, also includes non-restricted bank accounts and checks.

Cash equivalents are very safe assets that can be readily converted into cash, such as U.S. Treasury, savings, and money market accounts.

Accounts receivable consist of the short-term obligations owed to the company by its clients. Companies often sell products or services to customers on credit, which are then held in this account until they are paid off by the clients.

Lastly, inventory represents the raw materials, work-in-progress goods, and the company's finished goods. Depending on the company, the exact makeup of the inventory account will differ. For example, a manufacturing firm will carry a large amount of raw materials, while a retail firm carries none. The makeup of a retailer's inventory typically consists of goods purchased from manufacturers and wholesalers.

Non-Current Assets

Non-current assets are those assets that are not easily turned into cash and usually have a life span of a year or more. They can refer to tangible assets, such as machinery, computers, buildings, and land. Non-current assets can also be intangible assets, such as goodwill, patents, or copyrights. While these assets are not physical in nature, they are often the resources that can make or break a company—the value of a brand name, for instance, should not be underestimated.

Depreciation is calculated and deducted from most of these assets, which represents the economic cost of the asset over its useful life.

Types of Liabilities

On the other side of the balance sheet are the liabilities. *These are the financial obligations a company owes to outside parties.* Like assets, they can be both current and long term.

Current Liabilities are the company's liabilities, which will come due, or must be paid, within one year. This is comprised of both shorter term borrowings, such as accounts payables, along with the current portion of longer term borrowing, such as the latest interest payment on a 10-year loan.

Long-term Liabilities are debts and other nondebt financial obligations, which are due after a period of at least one year from the date of the balance sheet.

Shareholders' Equity is the initial amount of money invested in a business. If, at the end of the fiscal year, a company decides to reinvest its net earnings in the company (after taxes), these retained earnings will be transferred from the income statement onto the balance sheet into the shareholders' equity account. This account represents a company's total net worth. In order for the balance sheet to balance, total assets on one side have to equal total liabilities plus shareholders' equity on the other.

Reading the Balance Sheet

Many people have a natural aversion to accounting, but if you plan to become knowledgeable, you need to learn this rather easy task. Don't be intimidated.

As you can see from the balance sheet below, it is broken into two sides. Assets are on the left side, and the right side contains the company's liabilities and the shareholders' equity.

It also can be seen that this balance sheet is in balance, since the value of the assets equals the combined value of the liabilities and shareholders' equity.

Fig 1: Balance Sheet

Balance Sheet For ABC Corp. As of January 31, 2006				
Assets			**Liabilities and Shareholders Equity**	
Current Assets:			Current Liabilities:	
Cash and Cash equivalents	$	6,414	Commercial Paper	$ 3,754
Receivables		2,662	Accounts Payable	25,373
Inventories		32,191	Accrued Liabilities	13,465
Prepaid Expenses and Other		2,557	Accrued Income Tax	1,340
Total Current Assets	$	43,824	Long Term Debt due within one year	4,595
			Obligations Under Capital Leases due within one year	299
Property and Equipment, at Cost:			Total Current Liabilities	$ 48,826
Land	$	16,643		
Buildings and Improvements		56,163	Long Term Debt	$ 26,429
Fixtures and Equipment		22,750	Long Term Obligations Under Capital Leases	3,742
Transportation Equipment		1,746	Deferred Income Taxes and Other	4,552
Total Property and Equipment, at Cost	$	97,302	Minority Interest	1,467
			Total Long Term Liabilities	$ 36,190
Less Accumulated Depreciation		(21,427)	Shareholders' Equity:	
Total Property and Equipment, net	$	75,875	Preferred Stock	$ -
			Common Stock	417
Property Under Capital Lease		5,578	Capital in Excess of Par Value	2,596
Less Accumulated Amortization		(2,163)	Accumulated Comprehensive Other Income	1,053
			Retained Earnings	49,105
Property Under Capital Lease, net		(3,415)		
Goodwill		12,188	Total Shareholders' Equity	$ 53,171
Other Assets and Deferred Charges		2,885		
			Total Liabilities and Shareholders' Equity	
Total Assets	$	138,187		$ 138,187

Another interesting aspect of the balance sheet is how it is organized. The assets and liabilities sections of the balance sheet are organized by the current status of the account. So for the asset side, the accounts are classified typically from most liquid to least liquid. For the liabilities side, the accounts are organized from short-to long-term borrowings and other obligations.

How to Analyze the Balance Sheet By Using Ratios

With a better understanding of the balance sheet and how it is constructed, we can now consider some of the techniques used to analyze the information contained within the balance sheet. The most common technique is through financial ratio analysis.

This method uses formulas to analyze the company and its operations. For the balance sheet, using financial ratios (like the debt-to-equity ratio) can give you a better idea of the company's financial condition, along with its operational efficiency. It is important to note that some ratios will need information from more than one financial statement, such as from the balance sheet and the income statement.

The main types of ratios that use information from the balance sheet are financial strength ratios and activity ratios.

Financial strength ratios, such as the working capital and debt-to-equity ratios, provide information on how well the company can meet its obligations and how much they are leveraged. This can give investors an idea of how financially stable the company is and how the company finances itself. Activity ratios focus mainly on current accounts to show how well the company manages its operating cycle (which includes receivables, inventory, and payables). These ratios can provide important information about the operational efficiency of the company.

22

A wide range of individual financial ratios are also used by investors to learn more about a company.

Current Ratio

Perhaps the most important ratio, the current ratio is used to test the short-term liability-paying ability of a business. *It's calculated by dividing the total current assets by total current liabilities* in a company's most recent balance sheet. From the following data:

> **Total Current Assets divided**
> **by Total Current Liabilities**
> **Equals Current Ratio**

Current Ratio = Total Current Assets / Total Current Liabilities

Figure 2: Statements of Business

Financial Statements Of Business

Income Statement For Year

Sales Revenue	$ 1,040,000
Cost of Goods Sold Expense	6,760,000
Gross Margin	$ 3,640,000
Operating Expenses	2,080,000
Depreciation Expense	260,000
Operating Earnings	$ 1,300,000
Interest Expense	103,000
Earnings Before Income Tax	$ 1,197,000
Income Tax Expense	476,800
Net Income	$ 718,200
Earnings per Share	$ 3.59

Statement of Changes In Stockholders' Equity

	Capital Stock	Retained Earnings
Beginning Balance	$ 725,000	$ 2,026,500
Net Income For Year		718,200
Shares Issued During Year	50,000	
Dividends Paid During Year		(200,000)
Ending Balances	$ 775,000	$ 2,544,700

Balance Sheet

Assets

Current Assets		
Cash	$	565,807
Accounts Receivable		1,000,000
Inventory		1,690,000
Prepaid Expenses		160,000
Total Current Assets	$	3,415,607
Property, Plant, and Equipment	$	3,000,000
Accumulated Depreciation		(800,000)
Total Assets	$	5,615,807

Liabilities & Owners' Equity

Accounts Payable-Inventory	$	640,000
Accrued Expenses		257,167
Income Tax Payable		23,940
Short-Term Notes Payable		625,000
Total Current Liabilities	$	1,546,107
Long-Term Notes Payable		750,000
Stockholders' Equity:		
Capital Stock (200,000 shares)		775,000
Retained Earnings		2,544,700
Total Owners' Equity	$	3,319,700
Total Liabilities & Stockholders' Equity	$	5,615,807

Cash Flow Statement For Year

Cash Flows From Operating Activities

Net Income	$ 718,200
Accounts Receivable Increase	(175,000)
Inventory Increase	(440,000)
Prepaid Expenses Decrease	25,000
Depreciation Expense	260,000
Accounts Payable Increase	105,000
Accrued Expenses Increase	59,667
Income Tax Payable Decrease	(12,060)
Cash Flow From Operating Activities	$ 540,807

Cash Flows From Investing Activities

Purchase of Property, Plant, & Equipment	$ (750,000)

Cash Flows From Financing Activities

Short-Term Debt Borrowing	$ 25,000
Long-Term Debt Borrowing	150,000
Capital Stock Issue	50,000
Dividends Paid Stockholders	(200,000)
Cash Flow From Financing Activities	$ 25,000
Increase (Decrease) In Cash During Year	$ (184,193)

The current ratio for the company is computed as follows:

$3,415,807 Current Assets / $1,546,107 Current Liabilities = **2.21 Current Ratio** The current ratio is hardly ever expressed as a percent (which would be 221% in this case). The current ratio is stated as 2.21 to 1.00 for this company, or more simply just as 2.21

Generally, the current ratio for a business should be 2 to 1 or higher. If it's lower, find out why. Most businesses find that this minimum current ratio is expected by their creditors. In other words, short-term creditors generally like to see a business limit its current liabilities to one-half or less of its current assets. Why do short-term creditors put this limit on a business? The main reason is to provide a safety cushion of protection for the payment of its short-term liabilities. A current ratio of 2 to 1 means there is $2 of cash or assets that should be converted into cash during the near future that will be available to pay each $1 of current liabilities that come due in roughly the same time period. Each dollar of short-term liabilities is backed up with two dollars of cash on hand or near-term cash inflows. The extra dollar of current assets provides a margin of safety.

A company could remain solvent and pay its liabilities on time with a current ratio less than 2 to 1, perhaps even if its current ratio were as low as 1 to 1. In this example, the company's three non-interest-bearing liabilities—accounts payable, accrued expenses, and income tax payable—equal 27 percent of its total current assets. Its banker has loaned the business $625,000 on the basis of short-term loans, which is 18 percent of its total current assets. In most situations, short-term lenders would not loan the business too much more—although perhaps the business could persuade its banker to go up to perhaps $750,000 on short-term notes payable.

In summary, short-term sources of credit generally demand that a company's current assets be double its current liabilities. After all, creditors are not owners—they don't share in the profit earned by the business. The income on their loans is limited to the interest they charge (and collect). As a creditor, they quite properly minimize their loan risks; as limited-income (fixed-income) investors, they are not compensated to take on much risk.

Debt to Equity Ratio

A measure of a company's financial leverage is *calculated by dividing long term debt by stockholder equity.* This indicates what proportion of equity and debt the company is using to finance its assets.

Debt to Equity Ratio = Total Long-Term Debt/Total Stockholder Equity

Note: Sometimes, only interest-bearing long-term debt is used instead of total liabilities in the calculation.

A high debt/equity ratio generally means that a company has been aggressive in financing its growth with debt. This can result in volatile earnings as a result of the additional interest expense.

If a lot of debt is used to finance increased operations (high debt to equity), the company could potentially generate more earnings than it would have without this outside financing. If this were to increase earnings by a greater amount than the debt cost (interest), then the shareholders benefit, as more earnings are being spread around to the same number of shareholders.

The Quick Ratio

Inventory could take many weeks to convert into cash. Products are usually held two, three, or four months before being sold. If sales are made on credit, which is normal when one business sells to another business, there's a second waiting period before the receivables are collected.

In short, *inventory is not nearly as liquid as accounts receivable; it takes a lot longer to convert inventory into cash.* Further-more, there's no guarantee that all the inventory will be sold.

A more severe measure of the short-term liability-paying ability of a business is the acid test ("Quick") ratio, *which excludes inventory* (and prepaid expenses also).

Only cash, marketable securities investments (if any), and accounts receivable are counted as sources to pay the current liabilities of the business. It is also called the quick ratio because only cash and assets quickly convertible into cash are included in the amount available for paying current liabilities.

In this example, the company's acid test ratio is calculated as follows (the business has no investments in marketable securities):

$565,807 Cash + $1,000,000 Accounts Receivable divided by $1,546,107 Total Current Liabilities = 1.01 Acid Test Ratio. [1]

Quick Ratio =
Cash + Accounts Receivable/Total Current Liabilities

Generally, a company's acid test ratio should be 1 to 1 or
better, although you find many more exceptions to this as compared with the 2 to 1 current ratio standard.

To Summarize: The Balance Sheet
- The Balance Sheet is a snapshot of a specific day that shows the financial solvency of the business.

---

[1] AccountingInfo.com

- Current Ratio (Current Assets divided by Current Liabilities) should be close to or above 2.0.
- Quick Ratio (Current Assets less inventory divided by Current Liabilities) should be 1.0 or above.
- Get an accountant's opinion of the Balance Sheet.

Fig 3: The Operating (Income) Statement

The Operating Statement

1/1/01-12/31/01

		%
Revenue	$ 1,350,225.00	
Direct Costs		
Materials	391,565	0.290
Labor	272,745	0.202
Subcontract	263,229	0.195
Other direct	8,666	0.006
Total	$ 936,205.00	0.693
Gross Margin	$ 414,020.00	0.307
Selling Expense		
Sales Salaries	0	0.000
Commissions	0	0.000
Advertising	2,300	0.002
Other Selling		0.000
Total Selling	$ 2,300.00	0.002
G & A		
Officer Salaries	65,000	0.048
Admin Salaries	61,233	0.045
Other Admin Cost	94,440	0.070
Total G & A	$ 220,673.00	0.163
Total Selling + G & A	$ 222,973.00	0.165
Net Pre-Tax	$ 191,047.00	0.141

The operating statement (also known as the income statement) is the *most popular* financial statement. It is considered the "sexy" portion of the financial statements because it includes figures such as revenue, expenses, and net income.

In essence, an income statement tells you how much money a company brought in (its revenues), how much it spent (its expenses), and the difference between the two (profit/loss), over a specified time.

Profit is the reason companies are in business. While some new companies are not expected to be profitable for a few years, over the long run, no company can survive without profits.

The income statement is simply designed and is even simpler to read. The statement is looked at from top to bottom, with the top line listing the revenue (sales) brought in. Each subsequent line deducts expenses and costs from the revenue figure until you finally reach the bottom line (net income). Each item that has a line above the number means that it is a subtotal or total (the net income usually has a bold or double line below the number). The example given is a typical layout of an income statement.

There isn't one cookie-cutter way to present a company's income statement. The exact information presented depends, to some extent, on the type of business the company operates. Each line item is given a percentage of revenue, and each company has different percentages for each line item.

It's important to find out what's the typical net income for the industry *as a percentage of sales* before taxes, interest expense, and depreciation, and then compare it with your company.

It's also important to realize that the owner's salaries and benefits can be added to the net profit so that you can understand what the total profit is to ownership.

Also, if you are going to finance the purchase, you can add an expense item, such as "Annual Bank Loan Payment," and plug in the estimated payment and project what the net profit of the company will be after the additional financing expenses. As a matter of fact, the operating statement is the basis for pro forma forecasting.

If you still have a decent net profit after these additional expenses, you have the makings of a successful purchase—particularly if the company is capable of producing more profit than its current statement shows. That's why it's important to see what the company has done in the past and find out if and why there have been any significant changes.

To Summarize: Operating Statement

- The operating (or income) statement demonstrates the profitability of the company.
- Compare the net income before taxes, interest, and depreciation with industry standards, which you can obtain from industry associations or on the Internet.
- Compare percentages of revenue—not dollars. Percentages show a proportion of revenue, which can be compared from company to company and within industries.
- Add the owner's salary to net profit to determine total profit to ownership.
- Have an accountant review the operating statement.

If possible, try to obtain and then compare at least four years of financial statements to see what trends have occurred and ask questions about obvious large variations in line items.

How to Buy a Small Business
(And Let the Government Help Finance It)

Most businesses are priced based upon a multiple of total return to owner (net profit plus owner's salaries and benefits).

Once again, keep in mind that the balance sheet and operating statement show some important things:

- Has the ownership been running the business in a "professional manner" (using up-to-date financial statements and documenting policies and procedures)?

- How much debt does the company have on the books, and what liabilities may a new buyer be exposed to (particularly taxes!)?

- What assets will you receive with the business?
- What is the profitability of the business?

- An idea on how to price the business.

Financial statements can reveal many more important things, and it's best to have an accountant review the statement.

Many owners do not know much about financial statements and how to use them. They think all they need is an accountant, but this is only partially true. Make it a point to take a class or two about financial statements and how mangers use them to run a business. It's easy, interesting, and essential.

Numbers can be verified, but you have to be careful, and it usually requires that you be far along in the process of purchasing the business. *You should always have a clause in the sales agreement that allows you an "escape" if there are significant differences between what the financials show and what is reality.*

31

* Important:

It is extremely important that the buyer be held free from liability for any and all preexisting debt of the prior ownership.

Chapter 4: Determining Sales

Most businesses will have records that you can rely on to accurately show the profitability of the company (operating statement). Moreover, all should have income tax returns (if they don't, you might become liable!). If the seller does not have records you have confidence in, then you should have an agreement that allows you to work in the business for a period of time to prove the profitability.

If you do work in the business to determine profitability, the following procedures should be used to arrive at sales, cost of sales, gross profit, expenses, and net profit.

You must feel confident that the company is capable of producing a profit and carrying any loans you might need to purchase and operate the business.

It is essential to know what the company's revenue (sales) have been. Many sellers have sales tapes available to help substantiate sales; however, these are only as good as the honesty of the seller, and there is a better and more accurate way of determining sales.

As part of your sales contract, require the seller to allow you to work in the business for a period of two weeks to a month. In this way, you can verify sales each day and determine sales for a month and multiply that figure by 12. Then you will have a rough estimate of the yearly sales. If you want to be even more accurate, you can take the month's sales and then determine what percent of total sales each of the twelve months represent.

In the Northern states, if you calculate sales during the months of February or March, when the weather is extremely cold, you may get only 8 percent or 9 percent of yearly sales, whereas July and August could represent 12 percent of total sales.

How to Buy a Small Business
(And Let the Government Help Finance It)

Most small businesses have an industry organization that has key information, e.g., The National Association of Convenience Stores has a website, nacsonline.com, and the Restaurant Association has

January	7%
February	6%
March	6%
April	7%
May	8%
June	9%
July	9%
August	10%
September	10%
October	10%
November	8%
December	10%
Total	100%

Restaurant.org. If you just insert the name of the industry in the keyword section of your computer, most likely you will be directed to the appropriate website, and there you can find valuable information about the industry. After your research, you will have an example for projected sales, such as the one below.

If you are buying a business in August and you have monthly sales of $50,000.00 and you also know that August represents 10 percent of the yearly sales, then you can project the year's sales, or $500,000.00.

When you have your yearly estimate of sales, compare it to the sales the seller originally reported to determine how accurate his figures are. Always use your projections; they are probably more accurate, as there is a sound basis for the figures.

Making an accurate determination of sales is one of the most important steps in determining the economic feasibility of the purchase.

Chapter 5: Confirming Cost of Sales

In most retail businesses, the cost of sales is determined by taking an inventory of all merchandise or salable products at the time of takeover and pricing it.

If you are buying a bicycle store, for example, you would inventory all the cycles and parts by brand and then price each item by its cost; this would give you the total inventory cost. If you are working in the business for a month to determine the accuracy of the seller's figures, then you can use the following formula:

Computing Costs of Sales:

Opening inventory of sellable merchandise + *purchases* – *(minus) closing inventory = cost of sales*

Take an inventory of merchandise when you start working, add all purchases up to the date of purchase, and then take a final inventory and use the formula above to determine cost of sales.

Example:	
Opening Inventory	$30,000 Purchases
	+25,000
Closing Inventory	-28,000
Cost of Sales	$27,000

Many people complicate taking inventories. You don't have to be exact—just try to be as accurate as possible. I have seen people counting gum balls in a jar by taking all of them out and counting them one by one. If the jar holds

500 gum balls and it looks half full, you just estimate 250. If you are off ten to twenty gum balls, it won't have much effect on the *estimate* of final cost of sales. Your accuracy depends on the cost of the items involved. Missing ten cans of vegetables in a grocery inventory is not nearly as important as missing five diamonds in a jewelry store.

The idea is to be as accurate as possible, but don't be distracted by minor details. If you miss $200 in inventory, it probably is not going to have any serious effect on your decision to buy the business. When taking the inventory, be sure you have a methodical system in place—you don't want to take several aisles of inventory only to discover that you are not sure which aisle you have taken (don't laugh, it happens all the time!).

Make sure you are clear on the prices paid for each item in inventory. Many times the parties to a purchase/sale will agree to buy inventory on retail price less a given percent so they don't have to price each item individually. In the grocery business, for example, they may take inventory, price everything at retail, and then if the margins overall are generally 50 percent, they will take 50 percent of the total value, and that would be the cost basis for the sale.

Now that you have determined sales and cost of sales you are ready to determine gross profit.

If you follow the procedure we have outlined thus far, by the time you determine your gross profit, you should be feeling confident. You are beginning to know what you are buying. The next step is a simple one and will be easy to understand.

Chapter 6: Confirming Gross Profit

Gross Profit is rather simple:
Sales – Cost of Sales = Gross Profit

Example:	
Sales	$81,000
<u>Cost of Sales</u>	<u>- 27,000</u>
Gross Profit	$54,000

Gross profit percentage: Gross Profit/Sales
$54,000/$81,000 = 66.6%

This exercise also helps you to determine your cost of sales and your gross profit in both dollars and as a percentage. In most every industry, studies are available that indicate what the industry is attaining in sales, cost of sales, and gross profit.

Before making a purchase, it would be advisable to search for information on any available statistics regarding average sales, cost of sales, and net profit. Again, industry associations are a good source for this information.

Many times businesses are being sold because they aren't making enough profit, which can be due to poor management. If, for instance, you know the industry average for gross margin, you can determine the gross margin of the business and see how it compares. It could be as simple as the current owners not getting good pricing from their vendors.

Before purchasing a business, you must understand what the average industry numbers (percentages) are for at least gross margin and net profit. In fact, billions of dollars are made each year by savvy investors who know when a company is being mismanaged.

These "M&A" (merger and acquisition) specialists purchase a faltering company for pennies on the dollar and clean it up with good management practices and convert the loser into a winner … and then they sell the business for a whopping profit! Perhaps you will be just as successful!

Remember the old adage "buy low and sell high." This fact makes buying businesses an exciting experience. Always do your homework before you buy. Have an idea of what the "numbers" (gross profit percent and net profit percent) should be.

Chapter 7: Determining Operating Expense

Determining operating expense is more difficult than determining sales, cost of sales, and gross profit.

One of the best ways is to keep track of all expenses involved in the operation while you are working in the business. You can prepare a monthly operating statement, or budget, that you can follow to get a somewhat accurate record of operating expenses, and you can also project an average month's net profit.

Use the form 1A, Analysis of Income and Expenses, and fill in as many monthly expenses as you can. The seller should also be able to help you with the amount of monthly expense in each category.

Form 1A:

Analysis of Income and Expenses	
Gross Sales	$_____
Cost of Goods	$_____
Gross Profit	$_____
Expenses	
Labor	$_____
Tax Payroll	$_____
Depreciation	$_____
Commissions	$_____
Dues and Subscriptions	$_____
Rent/Lease	$_____
Rent—Equipment	$_____
Repairs and Maintenance	
	$_____
Telephone	$_____
Utilities	$_____
Trash and Rubbish	$_____

How to Buy a Small Business
(And Let the Government Help Finance It)

Advertising	$_____
Accounting	$_____
Insurance—Building	$_____
Insurance—Employees	$_____
Auto Expense	$_____
Auto Insurance	$_____
Supplies	$_____
Office Supplies	$_____
Postage	$_____
Licenses	$_____
Maintenance	$_____
Janitorial	$_____
Freight	$_____
Bad Debts	$_____
Bank Charges	$_____
Employee Benefits	$_____
Entertainment	$_____
Legal Expenses	$_____
Miscellaneous	$_____
Depreciation	$_____
	$_____
	$_____
Total Expense	$_____
Gross Profit	$_____
Less Total Operating Expense	
	$_____
Total Net Profit	$_____

At this point, you have determined what you can expect in net profit for a given month. You can now multiply this figure by 12 to get a yearly profit or, if you want to be more exact, you can refer to your analysis of the percent f sales by month and figure that the month you were working in the store was an 8 percent month and multiply other months according to their percentage of sales.

If you do a projection like this for each month of the year in advance, you then have a monthly budget. If at the end of each month you put your actual figures next to the budget figures, you can quickly see the areas where you are over or under budget and take action immediately. This is what management is all about: look at the numbers and make adjustments as needed as soon as possible.

Many companies do a budget month by month for a whole year and put it into the computer. Then at the end of each month, they record the actual figures and compare them to what was proposed. The computer only shows them the exceptions; they can then manage by only having to take immediate action on the exceptions.

As a reminder, the work of obtaining the information to prepare a profit and loss statement is only necessary if you do not receive sufficient or satisfactory information from the seller to feel comfortable in accepting the financial information supplied.

Chapter 8: Determine Which Employees to Retain

1. Your success in your new business could largely depend on retaining key employees as you take over the business.

2. A key employee could leave and open up a business in your trade area and siphon off a good deal of what business you paid for. Also, competitors may want to hire your key employees so they can attract some of your customers to them. Therefore, it is important that you have the <u>seller</u> obtain either *employment contracts* or *non-compete agreements* from his or her employees.

3. *If the business has been successful in the past, don't make any* immediate *changes in personnel. Follow the philosophy that "if it's not broke, doesn't fix it."*

Determine whether any salary increases have been granted since the last financial statement or cash flow statement or in recent weeks. Some owners selling a business want to gain favor with key employees while the sale is being negotiated, so they give them increases that are unknown to the buyer. If they have granted increases, it could change any financial statements you have been given.

It is also advisable to sit down with each employee and talk to them to get their input regarding the sale. You may learn a lot as to what improvements can be made to the business or you may find out about any actions recently taken by the current owner that would affect the business. You also have an opportunity to "size up your future employees."

Chapter 9: Verify Lease Terms or Appraise Real Estate

If you are purchasing property that is included in the business purchase, be sure you have the property appraised to assure yourself that you are not paying over market value. This includes equipment and any real estate.

You also have to follow all other necessary procedures when you purchase real estate:

- An estimate from the assessor as to what the new real estate taxes would be.
- It would also be advisable to have the real estate inspected to determine its condition before the purchase, particularly the roof and the electrical wiring.
- Determine property insurance cost.

If you are leasing the property, you need to obtain a copy of the lease as soon as possible and have it reviewed by your attorney. You certainly want to know the term of the lease and how many more years remain before its termination.

Some other leasing considerations include the following:

- Does the lease have any renewal options?
- What is the rent, and is there any future increase built into the lease?
- Can it be cancelled by either party at any time?
  I have seen leases with cancellation clauses that are not evident unless reviewed very deliberately. I once worked for a large company that had prepared a form lease with a carefully concealed 30-day cancellation provision that was approved by about seventy-five percent of the attorneys who reviewed it.

- Are there any requirements or additional payments necessary to transfer the lease?
- If possible, get the lessor's written agreement to transfer the lease. In many cases, particularly in shopping centers, the owner will require that they approve you as lessee, and there may also be a fee charged to transfer the lease.
- If the lease only has a few years remaining, make it a condition of your offer that the seller secure a lease extension or preferably a lease option to extend the lease.
- Also assure yourself that you are dealing with the owner, particularly if you are purchasing real estate.

Chapter 10: Review Any Equipment or Furniture Leases

Many business owners prefer to lease operating equipment or furniture; therefore, you should determine if any such leasing has been done and what are the terms, length, and amount of the lease. These amounts will have to be considered in preparing your operating expenses, which eventually will determine your net profit.

You also have to decide whether or not you want to continue to lease. In some cases, owners have leased equipment they are no longer using but are still paying rent on. This decision should be made before the final contract is signed. Moreover, a good addition to your contract is *"Buyer has the right to refuse and not be held liable for any leases that have not been specifically identified."*

Chapter 11: Check Out the Neighborhood

Over the years, many neighborhood characteristics change; some decline, some become more multi-ethnic, income levels change, or the neighborhood may be changing to more commercial or industrial. What may have been an excellent area for your business several years before may now be changing into one that will, in the near future, be a disadvantage. Traffic counts can rapidly change from normal to congested, or roads could be bypassed by new highways that would make your property obsolete. It's up to the buyer to find out; you can't depend upon the seller for this information.

If the business is located in a mall, be sure to check the vacancies, and inquire as to whether any anchor stores have moved out recently or are planning to move. Be sure no new stores are to be opened that would adversely affect your business. Competing retail stores are sometimes good because shoppers will do comparison shopping.

If you are purchasing a freestanding business, be sure that zoning allows for the type of business you are buying. Sometimes, property is zoned non-conforming and while the present operation can continue, a new owner might not be able to get permits.

Chapter 12: Confirm All Taxes

If you are required to pay property taxes on the premises of your new business, be sure you are aware of any changes in assessment as a result of your purchase. Many communities today reappraise sold properties and then reassess. In some cases, businesses were developed in areas where property values have "skyrocketed," but local laws restricted the amount of any increase in taxes by a maximum amount each year. Any new buyer, however, would be assessed at the current rates. So, it's best to check rather than be sorry.

When preparing your budget or cash flow, you are going to need to know your real estate tax obligation, withholding taxes, and any other license or tax fees necessary for the operation of the business. Make sure that all taxes have been paid before closing and that there is a clause in the sales contract that says "Buyer will not be held liable for any taxes owed by seller" (or something to that effect). Check with your attorney.

Chapter 13: New Competition?

A friend was going to buy a "pack and ship" store in a small strip shopping center. After meeting with the seller, just as he pulled out of the shopping center, he saw about three stores away a large sign in a freestanding store with the following notice: "Pack and Ship Store to Open Soon."

After inquiring about this store, he found out that it was a national franchise store that would provide many more services and at lower prices than the store he was thinking of purchasing. Should he go ahead and purchase the business, he could lose up to or in excess of 50 percent of the business that now existed.

Likewise, in malls, a new anchor store could move in that is much more diversified in its offerings and could be selling the same merchandise as the business you might be considering. If you are buying a wholesale or manufacturing business, be sure to investigate thoroughly if any new competitors are entering the market, which could dilute your sales.

Contrary to a store moving into the area also holds true when an anchor store in a shopping area or mall moves out. If a major store leaves, a lot of traffic could also move away from the area. People often form new traffic patterns and go to new areas to purchase products they once bought in the area of your prospective location, since they are no longer available there.

Chapter 14: Check All Equipment and Facilities

When you buy a new business, you should become familiar with the condition of any equipment or business assets involved in the sale. Be sure that any equipment necessary to the operation of the business is in good working condition and find out which equipment is still under warranty or extended warranty. If you need stoves, refrigerators, coolers, cash registers, manufacturing equipment, hair dryers, or any other equipment, they should be in good operating condition when you make the purchase so that you can immediately begin operation without any delay or further expense.

Facilities such as rest rooms should be operational, and floors, ceilings, booths, electric plugs, lights, and other things should be in good condition. These items can often be inspected by just "eyeballing" them; at other times, however, you might need a professional to do the inspecting.

Chapter 15: The Non-Compete Agreements

When you buy your small business, you would like to be comfortable knowing that the seller or some of his employees will not go into competition with you in the near future; therefore, it's important that you get a non-compete agreement from the seller, restricting them from going into business within a certain time period and within a certain distance from the business you are purchasing.

If the seller has key employees who, if they left, would have an adverse effect on the business, then you should require the seller to get non-compete agreements from those key employees.

Chapter 16: Licenses and Permits

Special licenses or permits are necessary for certain small businesses. In the restaurant business, food licenses are required. Convenience stores selling beer require an application and issuance of a beer license. Beauty shops require licenses, and licenses or permits are necessary for gasoline service stations, tattoo shops, cleaning establishments, donut shops, manufacturing, retail stores, and many more. In some instances, licenses are in force for existing businesses but will not be automatically issued for new businesses. Be sure that all licenses are available for your new endeavor.

Many manufacturing businesses may also require special licenses and government approval when new ownership takes over.

Be sure to investigate what licenses and permits are necessary for the business you intend to purchase and assure yourself before you make the purchase that the permits or licenses can be transferred or that new ones can be issued.

A waiting period is often involved in securing licenses; moreover, in some states, alcohol licenses require waiting periods after an application before you can begin selling the product. A six-week waiting period when trying to operate a restaurant without your liquor license can have a serious financial effect if you haven't allowed for it in your pro forma.

If you are remodeling, you or your contractor could need building permits and evidence of insurance before you begin construction. In many communities, the health department requires an inspection before opening a business.

Chapter 17: Insurance

The main purpose of insurance is to protect you against a potential risk or the unexpected. Protection for you or your business is necessary in the event of the death of a partner, a key employee, a lawsuit, fire, or any natural disaster. Some of the risks you should be insured against include the following:

1. Property Insurance should protect you from a number of losses, including the following:

   - *Buildings.* If you own the building where your business is operating, it should be covered.

   - *Business Property.* Any tables, chairs, operating equipment, counters, freezers, manufacturing equipment, anything not a permanent part of the building, as well as any improvements you might have made to leased premises.

2. Flood Insurance where needed and if available.

3. Loss of Income

4. Natural Disaster Insurance to cover hurricanes, tornados, and earthquakes, if these occur frequently in your area.

5. Workers' Compensation. It is required in every state except Texas. It pays for employees' medical expenses and missed wages if required while working. The amount of insurance employers must carry, rate of payment, and what types of employees must be carried vary, depending on the state.

6. Comprehensive General Liability policy to provide coverage for third parties who may be injured on the premises.

7. Auto Insurance to cover any company vehicles—e.g., liability, collision, uninsured motorists. If you are using a personal vehicle for business or if you have a company name on your personal auto, you should transfer ownership of the vehicle to the company in order to reduce your personal liability.

8. Health Insurance to cover your employees. Many people go to work for a company just because of the type of health coverage they may have, and many people stay in jobs that even pay less, just to not lose their health coverage.

9. Product Liability Insurance. All companies that manufacture, wholesale, distribute, and retail a product may be liable for its safety. Also, services may be capable of causing personal injury or property damage. Businesses are considered liable for negligence, breach of express or implied warranty, defective products, and defective warnings or instructions.

10. Internet Business Insurance. Internet businesses may wish to look into specialized insurance that covers liability for damage done by hackers and viruses. In addition, e-insurance often covers specialized online activities, including lawsuits resulting from meta tag abuse, banner advertising, or electronic copyright infringement.

11. Home-Based Business Insurance. Most home-owners' insurance policies do not generally cover home-based business losses. Home-based business insurance generally includes business property, professional

liability, personal and advertising injury, loss of business data, crime and theft, and disability.

12. Business Interruption Insurance. Some businesses may wish to acquire insurance that covers losses resulting from natural disasters, fires, and other catastrophes that may cause the operation to shut down for a significant period of time.

13. Malpractice Insurance. Some licensed professionals need protection against payments as the result of bodily injury or property damage, medical expenses, the cost of defending lawsuits, investigations and settlements, and bonds or judgments required during an appeal procedure.

It's advisable to contact a good general insurance agent when buying your business and then discuss what specific insurance you need for your business. These insurance costs can be sizeable and should be known before you decide to buy.

Chapter 18: The Sales Contract

Be sure to have an attorney thoroughly read the sales contract and pay particular attention to any places that are typed or written in.

When you review the sales contract, go to some quiet place, where you can read it without interference and can concentrate on each clause.

Most contracts provided by business brokers are standard contracts complying with the laws of the state; however, it's always good to read contracts to be sure you understand everything they contain. You don't want any surprises later on. Check the total price section and anything about down payment, any monthly payments, or interest rates.

If the present owner is doing any financing, be sure you calculate the total amount of all payments and interest so you fully understand what the total price is based upon. Ask questions and verify all the numbers.

If possible, be sure you have a commitment from the seller that they agree to work with you in the business for a period of at least two weeks to a month while you confirm the profitability of the business. *Make sure there is a clause providing for your money to be returned if the seller cannot confirm the numbers submitted to you.*

Make sure you can cancel the contract if the seller cannot prove their numbers to your satisfaction or if there is any other condition of the contract that is not satisfactory. Look for a provision that ensures your deposit and all monies advanced will be returned if the contract is not completed.

If the contract involves your signing a note, require that you have the right of prepayment at any time without penalty. Be sure any note contains the correct interest and payment period. If the contract is complicated, it would be advisable to have it reviewed by an attorney.

If the contract is typed rather than printed, you should insist on having your attorney review it. Most typed contracts are not necessarily proofread and could contain mistakes. It is always best to involve an attorney and an accountant to make sure that things are correct under state law. Some cost is necessary, but considering the stakes, you should do all the "due diligence" required by good judgment. After all, what may appear as logical might not mean that it's legal. You or a business broker should recognize your limitations.

Chapter 19: Selecting a Structure

One of the first decisions you should make when starting a small business is determining how your business should be structured.

This decision is so important that you are encouraged to consult an attorney for assistance. It's important to consider the following:

- How much control you wish to have
- The business vulnerability to lawsuits
- Expected profit (or loss) of the business
- Your need to access cash out of the business

There are several business entities under which you can conduct business. Some options for small-business owners include the following:

1. Sole Proprietorship
2. Partnerships
3. LLC Limited Liability Company
4. Subchapter S Corporations
5. C Corporations

Sole Proprietorship

A Sole Proprietorship means that you are doing business as yourself. Therefore, the limitations of liability enjoyed by a corporation do not apply to sole proprietors. All debts of the business are debts of the owner. A sole proprietor is a person doing business in their own name, and there is only one owner. A sole proprietorship is not a corporation. It does not pay corporate taxes, but the owner of the business pays personal income taxes on the profits. As a sole proprietor, you can register a trade name or "Doing Business As," so the owner can operate the business with a business name. Since a sole proprietorship means only one owner, the owner can make quick decisions without getting any other approvals. Tax returns are usually simple, and all profits of the business go directly to the owner.

Partnership

When forming a Partnership, a legal agreement should be in effect, setting forth how profits are divided, how differences can be solved, how decisions can be made, and whether one partner is more important in decision making. You also need a procedure for dissolving the corporation. Partnerships are often formed for financial reasons or because the strengths of one partner counter some weaknesses of the other. A written agreement should be made between partners.

Advantages of a partnership:

1. Business will benefit from partners with complementary skills.
2. Helps in raising funds.
3. Talented employees could be attracted to the business if they feel they can become partners.

Disadvantages

1. Sales decisions are shared; disagreements can occur.
2. Partners are liable for their decisions.

Limited Liability Company

The LLC is not a corporation, but it offers some of the same advantages. The LLC is advantageous to small-business owners because it offers the limited liability protection of a corporation with the "pass through" protection of a sole proprietorship. A LLC allows less ownership restrictions than corporations, and there is greater flexibility in business organization and management. While many owners think that forming a corporation is only for large companies, this is not true. The most important reason for incorporating is from the standpoint of personal liability protection. Also, if a sole proprietor dies, the business may automatically end or could become involved in legal entanglements. Corporations have unlimited life, extending beyond the death of their owners.

Subchapter S Corporations

A Subchapter S Corporation is a general corporation that has elected a special tax status with the IRS. Subchapter S Corporations are most appropriate for small-business owners who prefer to be taxed as if they were still proprietors. When a general corporation makes a profit, it pays a federal corporate income tax on the profit. If the corporation makes a profit and declares a dividend, the stockholder also has to pay income tax personally; this would amount to "double taxation." S Corporations avoid this double tax because all income is reported only once on the personal tax returns of the stockholders.

For many small-business owners, the S Corporation offers the best of both worlds, combining the tax advantages of a sole proprietorship with the limited liability of a corporate structure.

This election is something you should discuss with your accountant or attorney so that you can weigh the advantages and disadvantages.

C Corporation

A "C" Corporation is the most common corporate structure. It may have an unlimited number of stockholders, and this form of corporation is usually chosen by those companies planning to have more than thirty stockholders or large public stock offerings. A stockholder's personal liability is usually limited to their investment in the corporation. A corporation can be sued, taxed, or it can enter into legal agreements. The corporation has a life of its own and does not dissolve when ownership changes.

Advantages of a Corporation

1. Shareholders have limited responsibility for the debts of the corporation.
2. Corporations can raise additional funds from the sale of stock.
3. The cost of benefits given to officers and employees can be deducted.

Disadvantages

1. Taxes may be higher.
2. Dividends paid to shareholders are not deductible from business income; therefore, this income can be taxed twice.
3. They are monitored by federal, state, and local governments and may require more paperwork and records in order to comply with various requirements.

One of the first decisions to be made after a new business decides to incorporate is where to incorporate. For most small businesses, the answer is simple—register in your home state. If you conduct business outside your home state, then you may want to register in another state, which has corporation laws friendly to businesses, has a friendly state corporation code, reasonable costs of incorporation, and lenient information disclosure requirements. States with business-friendly laws are Delaware and Nevada. Remember, however, that unless your business is physically located in one of these states, you will still need to register for operation in your home state.

Getting sound legal and financial advice may be costly at the beginning, but it may save you from the wrong kind of structure and also save you from fines and penalties you did not know existed.

Chapter 20: Business Plan

What a Business Plan Can Do For You

As you start developing your business plan, keep in mind that the greatest beneficiary of this project is not your banker, investor, or accountant—it's you. A complete, thoughtful business plan is perhaps the best tool you can have to help you reach your own long-term goals, *but you will also need one if you are approaching anyone for funding, particularly your banker or the SBA.*

Developing a business plan enables you to do the following:

- Make the critical business decisions that focus your activities and maximize your resources.
- Understand the financial aspects of your business, including cash flow and break-even requirements.
- Gather crucial industry and marketing information.
- Anticipate and avoid obstacles your business is likely to encounter.
- Set specific goals and measurements to assess progress over time.
- Expand in new and increasingly profitable directions.
- Be more persuasive to funding sources.

Remember that when you buy or expand a business, more than your money and time are at stake. You risk your dreams as well. A good business plan helps you realize those dreams.

How to Buy a Small Business
(And Let the Government Help Finance It)

Four Steps to a Great Business Plan:

- Once you determine a business plan is a necessary tool for your company, you may wonder where to start. Because plan requires detailed in-formation on almost every aspect of your business, including the industry, market and operations, its preparation can seem over-whelming

The business plan process entails four fundamental steps:

- Laying out your basic business concept.
- Gathering data on the feasibility and specifics of your concept.
- Focusing and refining the concept based on the data you compile.
- Putting your plan in compelling form.

The first step is to lay out your basic business concept. It may be tempting to skip over this step, but if you wish to develop strategies for future success, you must first examine the assumptions underlying your current efforts.

Before you tackle the body of your business plan, you need information. So your next task is to gather reliable data relating to the different aspects of your business. Solid information gives you a realistic picture of what happens in businesses similar to yours, as well as a better understanding of your own company.

Only after you have compiled sufficient information and evaluated your business concept should you begin to try our plan.

Developing a business plan is much more of a business project than a writing assignment. The process itself, as well as the document produced, can positively affect the success of your business. During the everyday operation of your business, you do not have time to think through the issues you examine while you put together your business plan; the preparation process gives you a rare opportunity to enhance your knowledge of how your company, the market, and the industry work.

A thorough planning process gives you leverage to use when looking for money to fund your business, and an honest examination of your business concept increases your chances of success.

The Most Common Questions

Funding sources usually ask for answers to the following questions concerned with the heart of the plan:

- Is the business idea solid?
- Is there a sufficient market for the product or service?
- Are the financial projections healthy, realistic, and in line with the investor's or lender's funding patterns?
- Is key management described in the plan experienced and capable?
- Does the plan clearly describe how the investors or lenders will get their money back?

Within the first five minutes of examining your business plan, readers must perceive that the answers to all these questions are favorable.

Start your research by making a general statement that is the basis of your business and use the Research Questions worksheet on the following pages to record the general questions you have at this point and the issues you will investigate. How much information you gather will largely depend on your effort. This business planning process offers you an outstanding opportunity to better under-stand your business, the market, and the industry. Keep in mind that this process is a business activity and not a writing assignment.

Basic Business Concept

Is yours a retail, service, manufacturing, or distribution business?

_____

_____

_____

_____

What industry does it belong to?

_____

_____

_____

What products or services do you sell?

_____

_____

_____

Who are your potential customers?

_____

_____

_____

_____

Describe the overall marketing and sales strategy:

_____
_____
_____

What companies and types of companies do you consider to be your competition?

_____
_____
_____
_____

List your *competitive advantages, if any, in each area listed below:*

New Products/Services:

_____
_____
_____
_____

Improved Features/Services and Added Value:

_____

_____

_____

New or Underserved Market Reached:

_____

_____

_____

Research Questions

List the questions you will examine in each area of your business, using the categories below as guidelines.

Industry/Sector

_____

_____

_____

_____

Products/Services

_____

_____

_____

_____

Target/Market

_____

Competition

_____
_____
_____

Marketing and Sales Strategy

_____
_____

Basics of Operation

_____
_____
_____

Long-Term Considerations

_____
_____
_____
_____

Evaluating your Business Concept

This worksheet, which should be completed after conducting your initial research, helps you further refine your focus and determine whether your business is viable over the long term. In answering the questions, be honest and be tough.

Your Business Industry

How economically healthy is your business industry or sector?

_____
_____
_____
_____

Yes   No   Are necessary supply and support systems established?

Explain how your business/sector is sensitive to economic fluctuations

_____
_____
_____
_____

Yes   No   Are the forecasts for your industry or sector positive?

Your Product/Service

Yes   No   Is your product or service viable?

Yes   No   Are the costs of development prohibitive?

Your Market

Yes   No   Is your market clearly identifiable?

Yes   No   Is your market large enough to support your business?

Yes   No   Is your market too large and the costs to reach it prohibitive?

Yes   No   Is your market growing or remaining stable?

Yes   No   Is your market ready?

Yes   No   Is there a competitor with "deep pockets" who can drive you out?

Yes   No   Do customers have strong loyalty to existing companies?

Your Competition

How formidable is your competition?

_____

_____

_____

Yes   No   Do one or two competitors dominate the field?

Yes   No   Is the market share widely distributed?

What barriers to market entry will future competitors have?

_____

_____

_____

Your Suppliers/Distributors

How close are you to sources of supply?

_____

_____

_____

_____

How reliable are your suppliers or distributors?

_____

_____

Yes   No   Are you dependent on one or two suppliers or distributors?

Yes   No   Are your suppliers/distributors well established and dependable?

Your Operation Concerns

Yes   No   Does your business entail unusual or difficult operational problems? If so, describe them.

_____

_____

_____

Yes   No   Will personnel be hard to find, retain, or train?

Yes   No   Will you need to maintain large, expensive inventories?

Yes   No   Does new technology exist that will help you reduce costs?

Your Insurance Concerns

Yes   No   Are you able to secure the necessary insurance?

Yes   No   Is there a significant liability issue?

Yes   No   Will you have to carry heavy insurance premiums?

Your Financial Concerns

Describe any financial problems you anticipate

_____

_____

Yes   No   Is overhead unusually high, thus putting extra pressure on cash flow?

Yes   No   Will credit be hard to establish?

Yes   No   Are profit margins narrow, making the business vulnerable?

Yes   No   Will you have to carry a large amount of debt?

Yes   No   Do the principals have the expertise necessary?

Yes   No   Will ongoing training be necessary?

Yes   No   Are there any rapid technological changes that could affect costs and competitiveness?

Yes   No   Is the industry or market changing rapidly?

Yes   No   Are there any demographic or sociological factors likely to change the market?

Yes   No   Will it be costly to retain additional experts?

How Your Business Plan is Read

When evaluating a business plan, experienced plan readers spend the first five minutes reviewing it in this order: Executive Summary, Financials, Management; exit plan and/or terms of the deal, if applicable.

Funding sources primarily look for answers to the following questions concerned with the heart of the plan:

- Is the business idea solid?
- Is there a sufficient market for the product or service?
- Are the financial projections healthy, realistic, and in line with the investor's or lender's funding patterns?
- Is key management described in the plan experienced and capable?
- Does the plan clearly describe how the investors or lenders will get their money back?

Within the first five minutes of looking at your business plan, readers must perceive that the answers to all these questions are favorable.

A business plan is essentially a map to your targeted destination. Ideally, it gets you from your starting point to your goal, from your basic business concept to a healthy, successful business. It gives you a clear idea of the obstacles that lie ahead and points to alternate routes.

At this point, you are ready to proceed with your business plan. If you want to do it the easy way, have it looked at by a professional, and where you can be walked through the whole plan. Then you can go to www.bplans.com, where you can buy a business plan program for about $99.00 and be guided through the whole process. You will be most rewarded, though, by doing all the research and then writing the complete plan yourself, as you will then know your business and your competition better.

How to Buy a Small Business
(And Let the Government Help Finance It)

There are many ways a business plan can be written, and all of them could be valid.

To have a least one guide to follow in preparing one, however, we will outline a sample plan for you in this chapter.

The Business Plan is divided into six sections.

1. Executive Summary
2. Business Overview
3. Marketing
4. Management
5. Finances
6. Exit Strategy

1. Executive Summary
   At the very beginning of the plan, you should have an Executive Summary, which should be written last. This Executive Summary should be short and to the point, no more than two pages, but give the reader a complete picture of what you are trying to do, what financial help you need, if any, your market niche, your objectives, mission, and why your business will be successful. At the end of your business plan, you should include all supporting documents and financial information. Now let's consider the other five sections of the business plan.

2. Business Overview

   a. Why you are in business and your business goals.

    b. Company name, legal form, what you need to establish your business, and where the funds are coming from

3A. Marketing

    a. Describe your business and the general condition of the market
    b. Identify your target market
    c. Describe your competition and its strengths and weaknesses
    d. Customer profile

3B. Marketing—Products
and/or services

    a. Describe products or services
    b. Competitive advantages/disadvantages
    c. Why your products or services will sell

3C. Marketing and Sales
Strategy

    a. Customer profile
    b. How you will compete
    c. Pricing strategy
    d. How you reach customers
    e. Sales Tactics—personal selling versus advertising
    f. Promotion Strategy—describe other ways you are promoting your business

4.   Management
Background and experience of the principals or others will enable the owner to make a success of the business.

5.   Finances

6.   New Company

    1) Estimated P & L or Budget projections
    2) Initial start-up expense
    3) Current proposed Balance Sheet

  a. Existing Company
    1) Income Statement (3 years)
    2) Balance Sheet (3 years)
    3) Cash Flow Statement (12 months)
    4) Tax Returns and Financial Statements for the past three years
    5) Break-even Analysis Another tool for management decision making is called break-even analysis.

Once you know what your fixed costs will be, as well as the profit per unit sales or gross profit per sales $, you can determine the volume of sales needed to at least cover all your costs. You can also use the break-even formula to compute the break-even point if you are purchasing new equipment or real estate. Your break-even point can be determined by using the following formula:

- Sales price per unit – cost per unit = margin per unit

- Fixed costs divided by margin per unit = break even

Let's assume we operate a convenience store and our fixed costs are $200,000 a year, and we gross 35% on every $1.00 of sales revenue. Dividing the fixed cost of $200,000 by the contribution on sales of 35 cents reveals that the convenience store will break even with sales of approximately $571,403 per year or $47,617 per month. When the sales exceed $571,403 a year or $47,617 in a given month, the business will produce a profit. Sales below that point will produce a loss. The mix of items you sell will also affect your profitability. While your mix

77

may equal 35 percent gross profit, some items may contribute 50 percent. By increasing the sales of 50 percent items, you will increase your gross profit and lower your break-even point.

Now we are ready to put the business plan together for review by lenders and the SBA. A template for the organization of that business plan is given below. Let's start with the cover page, followed by a confidentiality agreement, table of contents, and the balance of the business plan.

How to Buy a Small Business
(And Let the Government Help Finance It)

ABC COMPANY

Business Plan
December 1, 2009

NAME
Address
City, State, ZIP Code
Telephone Number
Email Address

Confidentiality Agreement

The undersigned reader acknowledges that the information provided by_____ in this marketing plan is confidential; therefore, the reader agrees not to disclose without the express written permission of_____

It is acknowledged by the reader that information to be furnished in this marketing plan is in all respects confidential in nature other than information that is in the public domain through other means, and that any disclosure or use of same by the reader may cause serious harm or damage to

_____

Upon request, this document is to be immediately returned to_____

_____

_____
Signature

_____
Name [typed or printed]

_____
Date

This is a marketing plan. It does not imply an offering of securities.

How to Buy a Small Business
(And Let the Government Help Finance It)

Table of Contents

How to Buy a Small Business
(And Let the Government Help Finance It)

After you have completed the cover page, confidentiality agreement, and table of contents, you are ready to add the balance of your business plan to the package, followed by the supporting documents.

Business Plan Tips:

1. Forecast conservatively and try to leave an extra cushion of cash in reserve.
2. Keep in mind your audience.
3. Strategy is the core of your business plan.

What lenders look for:

1. Good credit
2. Good character
3. Down payment
4. Business plan

A sample procedure for submitting your business plan to a lender is as follows:

1. Call the SBA's local office and ask what banks do most of the SBA loans.
2. Take your business plan to one of the banks for approval.
3. If you are turned down by the bank, call the SBA and make an appointment with one of their agents to discuss your loan and seek their guarantee of approval.

21: Let the Government Finance Your Purchase

As a business consultant, some of the most common questions include the following:

- The bank turned me down for financing. What do I do now?
- My credit isn't the greatest. Where can I go for financing?
- Are there institutions other than banks that provide financing?

Financing your business and how the government can help you get the money to start or to buy your business will be addressed. We will also cover securing financing from Venture Capital, Brokers, and "Angels." When starting a business, sufficient capital is essential, as well as knowledge and planning to manage it well. Entrepreneurs need to avoid such common mistakes as securing the wrong type of financing, under-estimating the amount required for the purchase, or miscalculating the soft costs of borrowing money.

Each year over a million entrepreneurs and businesses use government loan programs to start or help grow their existing businesses. Who are the people who use these programs? They are the big and the small, the rich and the poor—people like Donald Trump, H. Ross Perot, and companies like Nike Shoes and Federal Express, not just the "little guy." Even George W. Bush and Dick Cheney took advantage of these programs before entering the White House. But not only well-connected "players" take advantage of these programs. In fact, most borrowers are indeed the "little guys" like you and me.

Raising capital is the most basic of all business functions, and normally it is not easy; in fact, it is often complex and frustrating. However, if you have planned effectively and done a good job of making your case, raising money for your business can go smoothly.

Lenders will ask many questions, including: What are your risks? How urgent is your need? For what purpose will the capital be used? What's the state of your industry? Is it depressed, stable, or is there growth?

Any lender will also require that capital be requested for a specific need, and you can obtain the best <u>terms</u> and conditions when you know exactly what your needs are rather than "just looking for money because you don't have enough." Perhaps more importantly, how does your need for financing mesh with your business plan? If you don't have a business plan, make writing one your first priority.

All lenders will want to see your plan for the growth of your prospective business.

So let's look at all the possibilities for financing your <u>proposed</u> business, and then we can select the method that best fits your situation.

Seller Financing

Having the seller finance the <u>purchase</u>—or part of it—is one of the most common situations.   Many sellers of small businesses will consider financing a portion of the selling price, even as much as 50 percent to 75 percent of the total purchase price.   Even if they are asking for all cash, there is nothing wrong in making an offer asking the seller to "carry some paper" for a few years.   You never know what a seller will accept until you try. In many cases, the seller doesn't have a particular place to invest the funds from the sale of their business, and you may be able to offer them better interest on a loan than they could receive from a safe bank investment.

After all, the worst that can happen is that they have to come back and run the business (and keep your down payment). Owner financing is frequently a "win-win" for both parties.

Self-Financing

Analyze your situation to see if you can finance your purchase with your own equity, such as savings, 401(k), or a second mortgage or refinance of your other assets. Lending institutions are fairly liberal on what they will lend on an equity loan, and the good thing about home equity loans is that they are tax deductible up to a certain amount.

If you have an IRA (Individual Retirement Account), you might use some of these funds, although there is a penalty for early withdrawal. Another source of funds could be the cash value of life insurance policies. The interest life insurance companies charge for such loans is often reasonable and may be less than other sources. *Be sure to check with a tax accountant before considering accessing any retirement or insurance investments you might have.*

Although borrowing from relatives, friends, and family is another source of financing, it's not one that I recommend. This sometimes alienates relatives and destroys friendships unless the loan is advanced after negotiating a *formal written loan agreement* that is satisfactory to both parties. It's advisable to offer some sort of security or some tangible sacrifice to provide some "recourse" if things don't go right. It shows good intentions and provides for some sort of accountability.

While credit cards are often used to finance business needs, better options are usually available because of the high interest rates involved. If the projected return from the business can conservatively cover the costs, however, then credit cards could be considered—but only as a last resort.

How to Buy a Small Business
(And Let the Government Help Finance It)

Bank Loans

Your next source of financing would be a bank. Before you seek any financing, be sure you have at least the following:

1. Business Plan to show how a proposed loan would be used (include a cash flow analysis for a full year's worth of operation)
2. A copy of the company's financial statements for the last three years (if possible)
3. Your personal financial statement

Any documentation of experience you or your key future employees or partners may have to show that you have the capacity to operate the business. If you don't have this information, you should have a plan to show how you are going to "make it happen."

Having these documents will not only help you get a loan but also help you take a good look at what you need to consider.

Some of the most common sources for debt financing are banks, savings and loans, commercial finance companies, and the U.S. Small Business Administration (SBA). Some state and local governments have also developed programs to help secure loans for small businesses, recognizing the positive effects small companies can have on the local economy.

Traditionally, banks have been the major source of small business debt financing. Their principal role has been to act as a short-term lender offering demand loans, seasonal lines of credit, and single-purpose loans for machinery and equipment. Generally, banks have been reluctant to offer long-term loans to small firms, but they are one of the principal sources for working with the federal government's SBA loan program.

Chapter 22: The Small Business Administration

The SBA is an excellent source for help in obtaining funds, and **this is where you can use the government to help you finance your business,** for both start-up and existing businesses. In many cases, the SBA loan requirements are less stringent than loans from commercial banks.

The SBA loan program is a well-managed effort of the federal government that provides help and stimulates the funding of small businesses seeking to secure adequate financing.

The SBA doesn't actually make loans. It *provides loan guarantees* to the banks, promising to pay back a certain percentage of the loan if you should fail to pay. The SBA will not only guarantee a loan but also help you prepare your loan package before you submit it to your bank.

The lender (the banks or savings and loans) actually provide the funds in an SBA loan and will still be exposed for a certain portion of the loan, and the lender will always be the principal contact for the borrower.

One of the more useful SBA programs is the "Low Doc Program," which is designed to increase the availability of loans under $100,000 to the small business community. It has been set up with the intention of helping to streamline and expedite the SBA loan review process. This is the SBA's "quick and easy program," a program offering a simple, one-page application form and rapid turnaround on loans up to $100,000. Furthermore, once an application has been completed, it is usually processed within just a few days.

The 7(a) Loan Guaranty program is the SBA's primary loan program. It is also the most flexible, since the agency can guarantee financing under the program for a variety of general business purposes.

How to Buy a Small Business
(And Let the Government Help Finance It)

To qualify for an SBA guaranty, a small business must meet the 7(a) loan guaranty criteria, and the lender must certify that it cannot provide funding on reasonable terms except with an SBA guaranty. The SBA can guaranty up to 85 percent of loans that are $150,000 or less and 75 percent of loans greater than $150,000. The maximum loan that the SBA can guarantee is $2 million, and the maximum guaranty the SBA can provide is $1 million. (See the chapter on the Stimulus Bill for recent changes effective through September 30, 2010.)

In guaranteeing the loan, the SBA assures the lender that if the borrower does not repay the loan, the government will reimburse the lender for its loss, up to the percentage of the SBA guaranty. The borrower, however, will still remain obligated for the full amount.

To get an SBA loan, you must *first have attempted* to *get financing from a bank or some other lending institution. If you haven't been successful, you may be eligible for SBA loan assistance.* Once you have fulfilled this requirement, you must prepare and submit the SBA loan application to an SBA-approved lender, which most often is a commercial bank. When the lender (bank) approves the application, it is submitted to the local SBA office. Once approved by the SBA, the lender approves the loan and disburses the funds.

One of the steps some buyers take to speed up the process is to be Pre-qualified for Business Purchase Financing before they buy a business. If you feel you are going to need SBA financing for your business purchase, it would be wise to be Pre-qualified before you even start the search process. This process can tell you, in advance, what size of business you can purchase, as well as many other factors about a potential investment.

How to Buy a Small Business
(And Let the Government Help Finance It)

Although limited in amount, SBA-guaranteed loans offer lower interest costs than nonguaranteed loans and are an excellent low-cost debt financing source for early-stage small businesses.

SBA-guaranteed loans are also the most common SBA loan and usually offer banks the following:

1. Loans to be made by private lenders are guaranteed up to 85 percent by the SBA.
2. A maximum guarantee of 85 percent for loans of $150,000 or less and up to 75 percent of loans above $150,000.

Information on small-business loans can be reviewed at the Small Business Administration website: www.sba.gov

If you will need an SBA guarantee for your loan, you should contact the SBA and speak to an agent and ask if he or she can advise you of what banks look most favorably on SBA loans.

The SBA defines a "small business" as one that is independently owned and operated and not dominant in its field. A small business must also meet the employment and sales standards developed by the Small Business Administration. In general, the following criteria are used by the SBA to determine if a concern qualifies as a small business and is eligible for SBA loan assistance:

1. Wholesale—not more than 100 employees
2. Retail or Service—average (3 years) annual sales or receipts of from $6 million to $29 million, depending on business type

You will also find a great deal of information on SBA financing, as well as grants from twenty-six government agencies, at the www.score.org website, which also has a lot of information on business plans. You should visit the SCORE website and review it thoroughly.

How to Buy a Small Business
(And Let the Government Help Finance It)

Chapter 23 Information Necessary for SBA

When attempting to obtain SBA/Bank financing, the following papers are required. Some of these papers will be in your business plan.

1. Application for loan: SBA form 4.

2. Statement of personal history: SBA form 912.

3. Personal Financial Statement: SBA form 413.

4. Detailed, signed Balance Sheet and Profit and Loss Statements current (within 90 days of application) and last three (3) fiscal years

5. Supplementary Schedules required on Current Financial Statements.

6. Detailed one (1) year projection of Income & Finances (please attach written explanation as to how you expect to achieve same).

7. A list of names and addresses of any subsidiaries and affiliates, including concerns where the applicant holds a controlling (but not necessarily a majority) interest and other concerns that may be affiliated by ownership, franchise, proposed merger, or otherwise with the applicant.

8. Certificate of doing business (if a corporation, stamp corporate seal on SBA form 4 section 12).

9. By law, the agency may not guarantee a loan if a business can obtain funds on reasonable terms from a bank or other private source. A borrower, therefore, must first seek private financing. A company must be independently owned and

operated, not dominant in its field and must meet certain standards of size in terms of employees or annual receipts. Loans cannot be made to speculative businesses, newspapers, or businesses engaged in gambling. Applicants for loans must also agree to comply with SBA regulations that there will be no discrimination in employment or services to the public, based on race, color, religion, national origin, sex, or marital status.

   a. Signed Business Federal Income Tax Returns for previous three (3) years

   b. Signed Personal Federal Income Tax Returns of Principals for previous three (3) years

   c. Personal Resume, including business experience of each principal

   d. Brief history of the business and its problems, including an explanation of why the SBA loan is needed and how it will help the business

10. Copy of Business Lease or note from landlord with terms of proposed lease for purchase of existing business.

   a. Current Balance Sheet and Profit and Loss statement of business to be purchased

   b. Previous two (2) years Federal Income Tax Returns of the business.

   c. Proposed Bill of Sale, including Terms of Sale

   d. Asking price with schedule of the following:

      1. Inventory

      2. Machinery & Equipment

      3. Furniture & Fixtures

Many of these items will be included in your business plan and be sure to include as many items as apply and that are available.

<u>Chapter 24 Venture Capital and Angels</u>

There is also a venture capitalist who arranges financing, and you can probably find some of these by inserting the words "Venture Capital" or "Financial Brokers" into the key word function of your computer. At one time, I wanted to buy an operating convenience store chain in upstate New York, and I was put in touch with a broker in New York City. I met him for lunch in Manhattan, and I took with me the last three years of financials on the business, as well as a five-year budget projection that I had prepared. I also included a copy of my resume, thoroughly describing my experience. After lunch (he paid), he told me he would get back to me within a week and let me know what they would do. True to his word, he contacted me within four days and offered to loan me the money to buy the business, told me the terms and conditions, and it was all very clear. One of their conditions was that they would receive 40 percent of the stock of the new corporation. While I didn't accept his proposal, I was impressed by his handling of the matter and the rapid response.

According to www.BusinessPartners.com, there are approximately one (1) million angels in the United States, and they are the leading source of real risk capital. Their website BusinessPartners.Com gives you the Angel Profile, as well as information on how to find an angel.

Chapter 25: Government Grants

While the SBA does not offer grants to start or expand small businesses, it can connect you with government resources for such grants. Visit their Federal Grant Resources page for more information. The SBA does offer some grant programs, which are generally designed to expand and enhance organizations that provide small business management, technical, or financial assistance. These grants generally support nonprofit organizations, intermediary lending institutions, as well as state and local governments.

At www.Grants.gov, you can apply for more than ninety different grants from twenty-six government agencies.

For more information on grants, go to www.sba.gov or www.score.org, or put Business Grants as your key word and click.

Chapter 26: Stimulus Bill

The American Recovery and Reinvestment Act contains a package of loan fee reductions, higher guarantees, new SBA programs, secondary market incentives, and enhancements to current SBA programs that are intended to unlock credit markets and begin economic recovery for the nation's small businesses. This program is effective June 15, 2009, and continues as long as funding is available or through September 30, 2010, whichever comes first.

"The tax incentives and credit stimulus of the Recovery Act will truly help small business owners affected by the credit crunch, and will provide financing opportunities to help them create new jobs in their communities" according to the SBA.

The bill provides $730 million to the SBA and makes changes to the agency's lending and investment programs so that they can reach more small businesses that need help. The funding includes the following:

- $375 million for temporary fee reductions on SBA loans and increased SBA guarantees up to 90 percent for certain loans.
- $255 million for a new loan program to help small businesses meet existing debt payments.
- $30 million to expand the SBA's Microloan program, enough to finance up to $50 million in new lending and $24 million in technical assistance grants to microlenders.

The bill also authorizes refinancing for certain SBA loans so borrowers can expand their businesses on favorable terms and also expands leverage capability for small-business investment companies.

How to Buy a Small Business
(And Let the Government Help Finance It)

This bill gives the SBA specific tools to make it easier and less expensive for small businesses to get loans, gives lenders new incentives to make more loans, and helps healthy SBA secondary markets boost liquidity.

The Stimulus bill takes a comprehensive approach and attacks several problems facing small businesses at once by reducing fees, guaranteeing a greater share of certain loans, expanding capacity in the Microloan program, providing new loans to help small businesses keep their doors open through economic hardship, as well as offering new mechanisms to help unfreeze the secondary markets for SBA-backed loans.

Declines in SBA lending volume in 2008, which are continuing in 2009, reflect problems in the broader credit markets and present hurdles to small businesses that are seeking credit in the current economy. The financial crisis has created a variety of conditions that impact small businesses, including a lack of liquidity in the banking system, a reluctance of many lenders to extend new loans, tightened credit standards, weaker finances at small businesses, and uncertainty about taking on new debt on the part of many entrepreneurs. The Recovery Act addresses small businesses' lending problems and investment and contracting issues. The bill helps small businesses' investment companies better leverage investment capital to reach more small companies. The bill also increases the current contract limit for the SBA's Surety Bond Guarantee program, which will help small businesses compete for contracts.

The bill allows the SBA to raise its loan guarantee from current levels to as much as 90 percent for some loans. At present, the SBA can guarantee up to 85 percent on loans up to $150,000 and up to 75 percent on loans greater than $150,000. The 50 percent guarantee on SBA Express loans would remain unchanged. Increasing the SBA guarantee percentage will encourage lenders to extend more capital to small businesses by increasing the share covered by an SBA guarantee.

The bill creates a new SBA loan program to provide deferred payment loans of up to $35,000 to viable small businesses that need the money to make payments on an existing, qualifying loan for up to six months. These loans will be 100 percent guaranteed. Repayment would not have to begin until twelve months after the loan is fully disbursed. The bill provides $255 million for this new program. These loans will help ensure that small businesses have time to refocus their business plans in order to succeed in the long run.

The bill expands the SBA's Microloan program, which provides small loans (up to $35,000) paired with technical assistance to start up newly established or growing small businesses. The bill provides funding to increase loans from the SBA to participating Microlenders by $50 million through September 30, 2010, and adds $24 million in grants to provide technical assistance to borrowers. Historically, these loans reach low-income individuals, women, and minorities in both rural and urban areas. Expanding this program through the Stimulus bill will help ensure these entrepreneurs are not left behind in the credit crunch.

The bill also gives the power to use the 504 Certified Development Company program to refinance existing loans for fixed assets, providing fresh support for small business expansion. This change will help business owners expand their current development projects and create jobs in their communities.

The bill authorizes the SBA to establish a secondary market for pools of "first lien" loans under the 504 program. These "first lien" loans from commercial lenders currently have no

How to Buy a Small Business
(And Let the Government Help Finance It)

SBA guarantee. The bill authorizes the SBA to deploy federal guarantees for pools of these first lien loans so that they can be sold to investors in a secondary market, providing liquidity for these first mortgages. This will help encourage lenders to continue participating in the SBA's 504 loan program, which provides a key source of capital for community development and other projects.

The bill also empowers the SBA to set up a Secondary Market Lending Authority that would make direct loans to broker-dealers that participate in the secondary market for SBA-backed loans from commercial lenders, assemble them into pools, and sell them to investors in the secondary loan market. This program may help address some of the issues facing the secondary market for SBA loans and may help SBA lenders make new loans to borrowers.

The bill helps SBA-licensed small-business investment companies (SBICs) and families of SBIC funds better leverage the capital they use to invest in small businesses. The bill sets maximum levels of funding the agency can provide to these companies at up to three times the private capital raised by those companies, or $150 million, whichever is less. It also raises the percentage any one SBIC can invest in a single small business to 10 percent of total capital and raises from 20 percent to 25 percent the percentage of any licensee's dollar investments that must be made in "smaller" businesses.

The bill also raises the maximum contract amount that can be covered by an SBA-guaranteed surety bond from $2 million to $5 million and under certain circumstances for contracts amounting to $10 million. It also provides additional funds to cover the costs of expanding this program. Small businesses need surety bonds in order to bid on and obtain many federal and other contracts. The SBA guarantees surety bonds to small businesses that private surety companies would not otherwise be able to extend.

Chapter 27: Helping Small Business Grow

The new Recovery Act will provide up to $15 billion to help unlock the secondary markets for small-business loans. By purchasing these securities, the Treasury Department will facilitate the ability of lenders to make new loans to small businesses by providing confidence that there will be a ready buyer for those loans in the secondary market.

In addition, the Small Business Administration is immediately implementing two key provisions of the Recovery Act—temporarily eliminating certain loan fees and raising guarantee levels on some of its loans. These steps will provide lenders with the security they need to start lending again to the millions of small-business owners desperately in need of capital.

Finally, the Treasury Department issued a call for new reporting requirements designed to better track small-business lending by banks and unveiled guidance from the IRS for an expanded "carryback" provision that will offer many small businesses a tax refund.

Here are some typical questions that may be asked about the Recovery Act.

Why will purchasing securities on the secondary market help small business?

Under normal circumstances, many banks sell a portion of their loans to companies that pool them together and sell them as securities to investors. The result is that the secondary markets significantly increase the amount of lending banks can offer to small business.

Over the last year, however, the secondary market for 7(a) and the first lien 504 securities have slowed considerably.

The institutions that securitize these loans have been unable to find buyers for the securities they have already packaged. This, in turn, has reduced their willingness to purchase new loans from banks. Since banks depend on the secondary markets for liquidity, they have become increasingly reluctant to extend credit to small businesses.

This new program will help unlock secondary markets by providing assurances that the government will stand ready to purchase 7(a) and 504 first lien securities. If you apply for a 7(a) or 504 loan at your local community bank, that bank will be more willing to lend because it will have confidence that the Treasury Department will be a ready buyer of the loan in the secondary markets.

The SBA will temporarily eliminate fees for borrowers and third-party lenders on its 504 Certified Development Company loans. These loans offer growing small businesses long-term fixed rate financing for major fixed assets, such as land, buildings, machinery, and equipment. These loans are aimed at fostering community development, creating jobs, and encouraging modernization.

How do I apply for these loans?

Borrowers apply for loans directly with their lending institutions, including banks, credit unions, and small-business lending companies. The SBA works with thousands of small and large lenders nationwide, who evaluate loan applications under their lending standards and decide whether to:

a) Make the loan through conventional financing, without an SBA guarantee, because the borrower meets their conventional credit standards.

b) Make the loan with an SBA guarantee if the borrower does not meet conventional standards and is eligible for SBA programs.
c) Decline to make the loan.

What kinds of businesses typically get SBA-backed loans?

Typical 7(a) borrowers are entrepreneurs looking to start, expand, or acquire a small business. In many cases, the applicant may have a strong business idea, management ability, and sound financial projections but have a shortfall in collateral to secure a loan or equity to put into the business.

In order to qualify for an SBA 7(a) loan, borrowers must be unable to secure conventional commercial financing on reasonable terms and be a "small business" as defined by SBA size standards. In 2008, of the $18 billion in SBA-backed loans, 35 percent went to start-up businesses, nearly 32 percent ($5.7 billion) went to minority-owned businesses, and nearly 23 percent went to women-owned businesses. The most frequently financed industries in 2008 were services, retail trade, accommodation, food service, construction firms, and manufacturing.

SBA-backed loans are three to five times more likely to be made to minority- and women-owned businesses than conventional small-business loans made by banks, according to a recent study by the Urban Institute.

Is there a limit on how much I can apply for?

The maximum loan amount for a 7(a) loan is $2 million. For 504 loans, the loan structures and amounts vary, since lenders and borrowers each determine how much equity they are putting into the loan. For the SBA portion of the loan, however, the maximum loan amount is either $2 million or $4 million, depending on the purpose of the loan.

For most purposes, the SBA's maximum guarantee for any borrower remains at $1,500.000, or 75 percent of a $2 million loan.

How soon can I get a loan to help me take advantage of these new programs?

You can apply immediately to any participating lender to take advantage of these programs.

- Fees will be reduced immediately for 7(a) loans
- Fees will also be eliminated immediately
- Microloan intermediaries are providing loans of up to $35,000 now to start up newly established and growing small businesses

Lenders will work with the SBA to process and approve these loans. Once the SBA receives a completed loan package from a lender, it can process the application in just a few days.

Is the elimination of borrower fees permanent and retro-active?

The temporary fee eliminations for 7(a) loans support an overall program level pf $8.7 billion, while the temporary fee eliminations for 504 loans support an overall program level of $3.6 billion. Depending on loan volume in these programs, the SBA estimates that it will be able to eliminate these fees on loans approved through approximately December 31, 2009. Fee eliminations will be retroactive for all eligible loans approved on or after February 17, 2009.

What if I had a 7(a) or 504 loan approved on or after February 17 and already paid the fees? How do I get a rebate?

The SBA is developing a refund mechanism and expects to be able to begin issuing refunds immediately. If borrowers have already paid lenders for the fees on eligible loans, the lenders must reimburse the borrowers from the SBA refund.

What kind of savings will I see from the temporary borrower fee elimination.

Fees for a 7(a) loan are based only on the guaranteed portion of the loan and depend on the size of the loan. The fees range from 2% to 3.75%.

As an example, a $300,000 loan with a 75 percent guaranty would have a guarantee fee of 3%. With the temporary elimination of fees, you would save $6,750.00 ($300,000 x 75% x3%). Under the new 90 percent guaranty, your savings would be $8,100 ($300,000 x 90% x 3%).

For a section 504 loan from a certified development company, the 1.5% application fee that is frequently charged to small businesses when they apply to the certified development company for a loan will not be charged. For a typical 504 loan of about $600,000, fee savings would equal about $9,000. In addition, the SBA charges the first mortgage lender a fee equal to .5% of the first mortgage in a Section 504 loan transaction. The SBA will temporarily eliminate that fee as well, further encouraging the first mortgage lender to get involved with the development project.

How to Buy a Small Business
(And Let the Government Help Finance It)

I am a small-business owner. What does the 90% guarantee mean to me?

It means that the lender will have less risk and a greater sense of security due to the higher guarantee percentage and will be more likely to extend credit to your small business.

Can I go to any lender in my area to take advantage of these new programs?

Only lenders who have been approved to participate in SBA lending programs can assist you with an SBA-guaranteed loan. Contact your local SBA district office to obtain a list of approved participants in your area. To locate the nearest SBA office, click on http:/www.sba.gov/localresources/index.html.

What if I have been already turned down by a bank in the past six months? Can I qualify for any of these new programs?

You are eligible to apply, but you will need to provide updated financial information that is current within 90 days. Over the past year, the financial position of many individuals and businesses has deteriorated, along with the economy, unfortunately making some no longer creditworthy.

The banks aren't lending to me. How do any of the announced programs help me?

Revisit your lender and specifically ask about the Recovery Act and SBA loans. Many of the provisions of the act provide incentives to lenders to encourage them to start lending again to get more dollars in the hands of small businesses that are most needy. Banks will now have access to more funds and higher guarantes, making it less risky and more attractive to lend to small businesses. Also, you can contact your local

SBA district office to obtain a list of SBA-participating lenders in your area.

I own a small business, and my revenue has gone down. The equity in my house has declined, and I don't have any more collateral to pledge. How do these programs help me?

The SBA does not have a specific level of collateral that must be pledged. If your business is viable and you have pledged all of your available business and personal assets, a banker may consider making a loan to you with an SBA guarantee.

Additionally, as part of the Recovery Act, the SBA is developing a new program to help viable businesses with immediate financial hardships. A short-term loan will be available to help them make payments on their existing loans. They are working hard to get this program up and running as quickly as possible.

The Recovery Act includes other initiatives to help small-business owners. This includes targeted tax relief for small-business owners, allowing "carryback" of losses from this year for up to the previous five years, reducing the estimated tax payments a small business makes to the IRS from 110% to 90%, and providing the ability to write off up to $250,000 of certain investments made in your small business.

I have been in business for two years and don't have three years of financial statements or business history. Can I get a loan?

Yes, you may qualify for a loan. SBA loan guarantee programs are available to start-up, newly established, and growing businesses. You will need to provide whatever financial information you have available and will also be asked to furnish financial projections with assumptions to support your loan request.

I was laid off from my job. Now I want to start a new business, building on my prior skills. I have a good business plan, and I am working with an accountant and an advisor. Can I get a loan from any of these new programs?

SBA loan programs are available to start-up businesses, as well as those that are already established. All applicants must meet certain SBA eligibility and credit requirements. In general, you must be organized for profit, meet SBA-specific size standards, and be unable to obtain funding on reasonable terms through traditional funding channels. When applying for a loan, you must prepare a written loan proposal or business plan. The proposal should outline your business strategy over the next several years and briefly explain who you are, your business background, the nature of your business, the amount and purpose of your loan request, your requested terms of repayment, how the funds will benefit your business, and how you will repay the loan.

The SBA has a host of resource partners (http://www.sba.gov/localresources/index.html) that can assist you in developing your plan, as well as online training resources through the Small Business Training Network. (http:/www.sba.gov/services/training/index.html)

I need working capital now to buy inventory and to make payroll. How long will it take to get a loan? How much can I apply for?

You can apply for a loan by talking to a local SBA participating lender. Once the SBA receives a complete application package from your lender, it typically responds to the lender within a few business days. SBA loan programs are available for most sound business purposes, including working capital, machinery and equipment, furniture and fixtures, land and building (including purchase, renovation and new   improvements, and debt financing (under special conditions). The maximum loan size under the SBA's 7(a) loan program is $2,000,000, although some programs have specific maximums that are lower.

I operate my business from home. Does that matter? Can I qualify for a loan?

It does not matter. A home-based business must still meet the standard eligibility and credit criteria for all businesses. If you meet all eligibility and credit criteria, you can apply for a loan.

What steps should I take to secure an SBA loan?

1. First, you should prepare a business plan, including all your business projections.
2. Contact your local SBA district office to obtain a list of approved lenders in your area.
3. Take your proposal to the lender of choice for approval. If you are not successful, go to another lender. If not successful, then go to step 4.
4. Go personally to the SBA office and solicit their advice as to how to proceed.
5. Don't give up. Repeat the process if necessary.

Chapter 28: You Can Do It

At first impression, it would seem that there so many things to do before buying a small business, and t here is. But many of the important items can be accomplished very simply.

If you're buying a business in a shopping mall or on a busy street, in just thirty minutes you can walk the area, talk to a few of the businesspeople, and find out all you need to know about what is going on in the area. If you are buying a wholesale business, talk to some of your seller's competitors to learn about what's going on in the local market and pay attention to any gossip about the business you are considering.

Your business broker can help save you time and provide a lot of valuable information about the local business situation.

Moreover, he or she can give you some help in pulling together all of the information you'll need to make a good decision. A business broker can also be a vital link in communication between you and the seller. They can act as the custodian for such important documents as the company's financials, which most sellers are very reluctant to give to just any interested party.

Keep in mind that it is also a good idea to have a "go between" when entering into negotiations. This is more important than it might appear. Keeping emotions and person alities out of the negotiation process can really help facilitate a smooth transaction for both buyer and seller.

Some parting advice: Do your "homework" and take the long view. Owning and operating your own business may be one of the best and most important decisions you will ever make, and it shouldn't be taken lightly.

Reread this book and use it as a sort of "checklist" to help you stay focused on what you need to consider when buying your own business. This book covers very thoroughly two of the most difficult parts of buying or starting a business—preparing a thorough business plan and finding a source of financing.

I wish you success in your new venture.

INDEX

www.ingramcontent.com/pod-product-compliance
Lightning Source LLC
Chambersburg PA
CBHW051448280526
45785CB00003B/1477